Camping

Written by Gill Munton

Speed Sounds

Consonants *Ask children to say the sounds.*

f	l	m	n	r	s	v	z	**sh**	**th**	**ng**
ff	ll		nn		ss	ve	zz			**nk**
							s			

b	c	d	g	h	j	p	qu	t	w	x	y	**ch**
bb	k		gg			**pp**		tt	wh			**tch**
	ck											

Each box contains one sound but sometimes more than one grapheme.
*Focus graphemes for this story are **circled**.*

4

Vowels

Ask children to say the sounds in and out of order.

a	e	i	o	u
at	hen	in	on	up

ay	ee	igh	ow	oo
day	see	high	blow	zoo

Story Green Words

Ask children to read the words first in Fred Talk and then say the word.

van   trip   tent   lamp   cup   lunch   rod

grass   egg   drank   pop   pond   match   fun

Ask children to say the syllables and then read the whole word.

past|a   sal|ad   plas|tic

Ask children to read the root first and then the whole word with the suffix.

camp → camping   blanket → blankets

pan → pans   dish → dishes   fish → fishing

twig → twigs

Vocabulary Check

Discuss the meaning (as used in the non-fiction text) after the children have read the word.

	definition
plastic	a hard, man-made material
match	a small, thin piece of wood with one end that makes fire
supper	an evening meal

Red Words

Ask children to practise reading the words across the rows, down the columns and in and out of order clearly and quickly.

they	the	of
to	supper*	for*
what	ball	all
your	like	go

* Red Word in this book only

Ed and Dad went camping.

They went in Dad's van.

Things for the camping trip:

- tent
- lamp
- blankets
- pans
- plastic cups and dishes
- things for lunch
- fishing rods

They put up the tent.

Then they sat on the grass.

They had eggs and pasta salad for lunch.

They drank cans of pop.

They went fishing in a pond.
Ed got a big fish.

Dad got twigs and lit them with a match.

They had fish and salad for supper.

At ten o'clock they went to bed in the tent.

Ed and Dad had fun camping!

Questions to talk about

Ask children to TTYP for each question using 'Fastest finger' (FF) or 'Have a think' (HaT).

p.10 (FF)   What did Ed and Dad bring to cook food in?

p.13 (FF)   What did they have for lunch?

p.15 (FF)   What did Dad use to make a fire?

p.16 (FF)   What time did they go to bed?

(HaT)   What do you think Ed enjoyed most?

Speedy Green Words

Ask children to practise reading the words across the rows, down the columns and in and out of order clearly and quickly.

went	put	then
sat	on	had
got	big	fish
them	with	bed